THE BEGINNING JOURNEY

KJP ALLEN

THE BEGINNING JOURNEY
Copyright © 2021 KJP Allen
All rights reserved

Typesetting and cover design by FormattingExperts.com

ISBN 978-1-7366226-0-5

DEDICATION

This book is dedicated to my family and friends and those who tolerated me on and off the track. Many whom received a few of these works as gifts to be inspired by.

To Maryann McMahon and the One above who made it all possible for this journey to take place with the connections and encouragements.

To Aleah W who encouraged and helped define and refine some of my works to make them shine brighter.

Special recognition to Sister – Nicole, Niece – Renee and Nephew – Xavier. Included is a piece by my niece.

PEOPLE

MY SISTER

How do I capture you my little one!
I must capture the image before it is gone:
Sometimes you are like an egg, so fragile and brown,
But where it is pointy you are smooth and round.
Like an egg you are so easy to break
So, I handle you with love for your own little sake:
Other times you are like a kitten so frisky and bright,
And at the same time so soft so I snuggle you tight:

I would then hold you close, but my tears would flow,
Knowing you would not understand I let you go:
Then you are like a butterfly that flutters here and there
Investigating everything without thought or care:
Or you wander about like a little deer,
So agile and young, you frolic without fear:
However, you are not a deer but a little dear to me,
And my dear little one, I love you tenderly.

RENÉE

The joy of seeing you,
elevates my musical tempo when we meet.
Do you really see me? I ask myself,
as my heart slows to a softer beat,
like gentle Music to my ears.

I miss the carefree timbre of laughter,
that rose with dynamic abandon,
like the cadence of cicadas close to sunset,
Crescendo in my ears, only performed for me,
which was once harmonic, but not anymore!

All I see now are the sad eyes, staring at me silently:
Unspoken words: Unheard beats:
Where are the melodious sounds I once heard?
Are they extinguished? Or are they silenced?

It is as though you pressed the mute button.
I try to tune in, but the frequency is no longer there.
Where has the Rhythm gone?
Why has it changed so much, that I cannot find it?
You are silent, that is why I cannot hear it.

SUSAN & JUSTIN

May the tides of time be joyful and rewarding to both of you,
for this union is one of commitment and work that requires two.
Always try to listen and learn from what each other has to say,
to be understood, you both must prepare the way.

Remember to be supportive as often as you both can,
for life can be challenging and frustrating which may get out of hand.
Realize that respect and trust is to be added along the way,
to avoid unhappy moments when tempers tend to display.

Increase patience and be willing to compromise,
for not all things are rosy and perfect as you once realized.
Admit to your mistakes, although it may be difficult to bare,
for each of you to learn, and grow, you both must care.

Give to each other the closeness, yet the space needed to thrive,
for knowing when to hold and when to let go comes with being wise.
Every day look for some Sunshine amongst the clouds that will appear,
to create the bright spot both of you must share.

XAVIER

I paint you because I can,
My young flower:
So different each day.
Energetic,
Bright,
So difficult to paint,
For your beauty varies in the light.

I capture you because I can,
My precious One:
Full of life in the day
Vibrant,
A delight
Your patterns, I must highlight.

DOC. MAC-G

To a wonderful individual so warm and true
Hoping that this season is a pleasant one for you:
And to a special person so dear and kind
Never stop being so loving and sincere all the time.
Kindness from you is always there for all,
You give of your time no matter when I call.
Only you can be so open, and patient and dear,
Understanding the pains, we tell for you to hear.
Do, be good to yourself this coming NEW YEAR
On occasion take time off to enjoy the fresh air
Continue to be caring, sensitive and carefree,
God bless you Doc for all you do and mean to me.

FATHER

I have lost you, which I once had,
When you were gone, I was incredibly sad,
Why were we ever not seen with each other?

The Reason: we were not supposed to be together.

We were so close in our relationship,
Yet far apart as two foreign ships
Why didn't we try and get to know each other?

The Reason: we were not supposed to be together.

Now that you left, I miss you a great deal,
If you were here, you will know how I feel,
Why could not we communicate with each other?

The Reason: we were not supposed to be together.

When I think of you, tears come to my eyes,
And I say, why did you have to die?
Why could not you stay here forever?

The Reason: we were not supposed to be together.

MOTHER'S

Mother's Day is once a year,
But we know that one day,
Is never enough for all that they do:
Their accomplishments are many,
And with little time
Many things must be done.

How do we show them once a year?
That on this one day
We want them to know,
That without their continued presence,
And the many things they do
We will not be who we are today.

Mothers, celebrate this day,
With honor and hope
Knowing that you are thought of,
On more days that this one
And always will be recognized,
Every single day of the year.

DENTIST

I wanted to show my gratefulness to you with a prose,
For helping to relieve my dental stress that arose:
You have given so much of your time and care,
Into keeping my troublesome teeth in good repair.

I know that you have been helping others for quite a while,
Because of your concerned nature and your professional style,
It is reflected in your patience and calmness,
And in the expert way you never seem to digress.

Sometimes many patients enter and leave,
And they thank you many times for their painful relief,
But I, on the other hand have been constantly there,
Which is why I write this momentous poem for you to share.

I cannot thank you enough for the time you have worked,
In helping to correct my problems wherever they Lurked,
May the benefits that you receive be bountiful and plenty,
To compensate for your skills which are extraordinary.

MY LOVE

My love for you comes from my depths,
Where no hands can reach, and no eyes can see:
Only my heart and mind can control and reveal it,
Through my touch, words, and actions to you.

My love is mature and real, warm, and sensitive,
To be given openly if you desire it:
My love if you would share it, is to be used wisely,
For there are passions to be disturbed and discovered.

I know not yet what my capabilities of love are,
Neither do I know how far I can extend it,
Or how much I can take,
For my love for you is all that I have, to give.

MOMENTS

I remember,
The moments we shared,
Are ours to retain,
Ours to reminisce,
And ours not to forget.

I recall,
The hesitating at first
The trembling touch,
The assertiveness
And the confidence that followed.

In time,
We gave of ourselves:
The knowledge we had,
The understanding
And the unselfish love.

In return,
We accepted with openness,
New experience
Different values
And mutual affection.

The patience
We took with each other,
We built with love,
Withstood obstacles
And gave it all we had.

What I remember
No one can duplicate,
Nor can they erase,
What took place,
Nor will they come close.

WE KNOW

We know there are those who give,
And there are those who take,
Yet in between, there are those who live,
To do deeds others appreciate.

One aspires to lead not to be led,
When others tend to follow the light,
Yet in the midst, of getting ahead,
They find the time to make things right.

They venture forth with the good deed,
And doing it with a sense of pride,
Not worrying about how much you need,
And are rewarded for the feats they provide.

You, are one of those few who are rare,
That guides, assists, and directs,
In spite, of the many things in your care
You provide more than one expects.

NICE

So many people are so nice and kind to me,
That at times I feel so happy and free:
They treat me with such love and special care,
That at times I say a thankful prayer,,
I did not know such people existed is the real world,
That at times I think "OH" what I missed as a little girl.
They even help and comfort me,
That at times my tears run freely.
These people do the same for others like me,
That at times I feel some jealously:
They care and love for everyone differently,
That at times I am happy they spared some time for me.

BE CONTENT

Would you be content,
With the simple things I show
Would you have the time to watch me,
No matter which direction I go?
You see, I have no eyes to gaze upon you,
To admire you when you are not within my reach,
To follow your every step when you move.
Neither do I have the ears to hear you
To listen intently to the things you say,
To be rippled by the sound of yours voice
And be swayed in every way.
Nor will you be able to hold me,
Or care about me,
For you see, I am who I am:
However, will reassure your doubts,
In whatever, ways I can
When you are sad, in need of comfort,
Do not hesitate, come and be near me,
Blend your tears with mine
So that I can share in your melancholy:
Allow them to flow freely.
Let them gush blindly over,
Releasing the unwanted aches truly.
Should you become fatigued and troubled,
Permit me to restore your strength,
And bestow you with new energy,
Do not rush, bide yourself gently,
So, I can erase your pains,
While we have the opportunity.

SPECIAL

To be special,
you must believe:
That you are above all
An individual with potential
Not yet unleashed within this realm:

As a special person,
you must be seen:
Who you are amongst others,
That individual with untapped inner drive
Not yet mastered not yet grasped:

This special person,
who you are:
One who manages the impossible
The individual with self esteem
Not yet recognized, but easily understood:

Be that special person,
at all times:
The one who rises to the top
An individual granted with the gift,
That is recognized and to be dispersed

I WANT TO SHARE

I wanted to share something special with you,
Something that is different but treasured by few:
It is a prose that comes from deep in the heart,
A kind of gift that cannot be bought:

Each day our lives appear faster than before,
With less and less time to share and do more,
We want what is best, so we strive for it all,
Forgetting the little things, we use to recall:

Where has the time gone when we strolled?
Now we move so fast we get out of control,
We do not stop or pause to reflect and unwind,
Our lives are a constant go, and on fast forward all the time:

We think that achieving more is best for our lives,
On the go all the time making a sacrifice:
Giving and helping without concern for the day,
Neglecting the true feelings, we lose sight and our way:

When are we to realize that life is a constant change,
One that does not flow smoothly but comes in waves:
We must ride the tides with the highs and the lows,
To experience the different effects and prepare for unexpected foes:

One must step back to appreciate things as they surface,
Overlook the flaws and bring other values into focus:
Enhance what we see for we are not a star,
That constantly shines day and night from afar:

See and experience life memorably each day,
It is because of the challenges that come our way:
We want to slow down and enjoy things before they go,
Yet, the time rages on and we are consumed by the flow:

Now I realize each day is one that is new,
So, I try to forget the pain that cause me to be blue,
I grab hold of the simple things that pass my way.
And block the big things that tend to lead me astray.

EMOTIONS

TO YOU I GIVE THIS

To you I give this
To care and understand
As though it were a child:
At the start be gentle
For it is unused:
Nurture mold and console it.
Give it what it needs:
Help it along,
And watch it grow.
Frequently it holds back:
It is unsure of itself.
Be patient, it will learn.
Occasionally,
It is headstrong,
It is impatient:
Be understanding,
It needs space.
Eventually it will reach out.
To share experiences:
It will open up,
To receive new ideas:
In time it will thrive
To be itself.

FRAGMENT

We are not a fragment of another being,
Considered like a missing piece,
Waiting to fuse with the other,
Combining to create a total.
We are each a whole:
Separate together and complete,
That can link together like a chain,
Allowing ourselves space to expand
Forming bonds when we join.
Bonds that are secure
To provide space to share and exchange,
But loose to permit growth and difference
With a capacity to include others.

I AM

I am like a flower:
That has just begun to bloom,
Into a beautiful being:
Come watch me unfold,
My tender petals.
See the way they
They slowly unwind,
Opening up
Like an awakening baby
Reaching out
Revealing the beauty inside.

PONDER I DO

Ponder I do,
About unveiling,
The emotions of love
The thoughts of passion
Craving to erupt
Simultaneously
When I see him.

Confronted I am,
With revealing,
What circulates within,
Stirring the senses
Triggering them off
Uncontrollably.

The blood heats:
Urging the heart.
The body tingles,
Desiring to embrace
Spontaneously.

The mind is willing,
To comply:
Yet the body
Hesitates,
Concealing
Not releasing
Instantly.

NO CLUE

They said I will find you, but they left me no clue,
They said that I would know you, but what am I to do.
Tell me who you are, so I can meet you:
Tell me where to look, so that I can know you.

I feel the cool wind, as I run each day,
I feel the welcoming air, as it cools me each step of the way,
When I stop to listen, the wind blows all around,
When I pause to look, I feel you but no sound.

I feel the water, as I watch the tide rush in
I feel the rays warm me, as I frolic and swim,
I watch the birds, as they glide closely to the top
I watch the waves, as it laps their feet when they stop.

Where am I to find you, now that I have been up and about,
When they said I will see you, I had no doubt:
I have looked everywhere, during rest and play,
I will have to try again another time, if you decide to grace the day.

HEAVY IS THE SOUL

Heavy is the soul that bears the burden when you are gone,
Heavy is the heart that needs comfort when the day is done,
Heavy is the mind that wonders, why so much pain?
Heavy is the feeling when I ponder about you in vain:

Did you know that my soul would grieve each day?
Did you know that my heart would ache when I pray?
Did you know that my mind thinks of you as I tear?
Did you know that I would have so much burden to bear?

I knew you had to leave but not so soon,
I knew you had no time, but I blocked out the gloom.
I knew you would be missed, but I was not prepared,
I knew you wanted more time, so I prayed and prayed:

Help me to deal every day with you not in sight.
Help me to be strong inside day and night.
Help me to reach the place where I can accept,
Help me to heal and remember but not forget.

Each day I face without you deepens the pain,
Each day I face without you remains the same.
Each day I face without you weakens my mind,
Each day I face without you is never kind.

Let me learn how to be at peace but keep you near,
Let me learn to heal with the pain I bare.
Let me learn to take things in stride and grow,
Let me learn that life is given and live before I go.

CONFUSED

Confused you are when you see me.
Is it because you are unsure?
What is it I do to confuse you?
I am understanding patient and sure.
Use your senses to reach me:
Reach out with your eyes and adore.
You will see that I am not that lonely,
I am warm and vibrant to the core.
Use your senses to reach me:
Imagine the sensations I implore.
You will feel the static charged energy,
I am alive with the vitality and more.
Open your senses and hear me:
For I am quieter more than before.
Know that my silence is not uncertainty,
I am aware attuned and sure.
Open your senses and taste me:
Enjoy the flavor as you explore.
Just like the taste of honey
I am sweet and savory and more.
Be confused no more as you devour me:
Let my mind soul and body soar.
Allow the pleasures to roam free,
I am the one who can make you roar.

THE RETURN

The distance without you have been lonely and low:
Like the desert without water
Like a mountain without snow.

Without you I have been empty confused and down
Like a captured animal
One that is not free to roam around.

What kept you apart for so long a time?
Without words or thoughts
Of how I wanted to create and rhyme?

You used to be there with words to flow with ease,
Like the soft white snow
Swirling around in the gentle breeze.

I missed the inspiration of your comforting words,
That blossomed like spring leaves,
Fluttering and swaying with chirping birds.

How I have missed your gentle and flowing style,
That escaped the pen with curiosity and flare,
To inspire the heart and enlighten the smile.

Thank you for returning and giving me the touch,
To Enable my writing to flourish and grow
To allow others to enjoy and treasure very much.

LET ME

Let me near you:
So, I can
Touch you, feel you, and share you.

I will let you show me:
How to
Warm you, comfort you, and calm me.

Let me hold you:
So, I can
Explore you, reach you, and console you.

I will let you:
Teach me,
How to please you, tease you, and reach me.

Let me unfold you:
So, I can
Understand you, savor you, and hold you.

I will let you:
Guide me,
To please you, to know you, and to console me.

THE WAIT

How long must I wait, to encounter you?
How long will you wait when I am away from you?

As I wait, I recall what we always go through:
While I lay and wait, and let the feelings race through:

Time we know will not wait, for anyone even two:
Who always seem to wait, for stolen moments or two:

You know that I must wait, for it is the only thing to do,
Knowing that you also wait, for me to accept as you do.

What comes to mind as I wait, for me to return to you?
Life is easier as you wait, for good things to come to you.

Bring to mind as you wait, as you say that it is true,
And do not mind that I wait, for the pleasures to come true.

How I love to prolong and wait, to know you enjoy what I do.
For the excitement is worth the wait, for the things we would do.

Each new day is a wait, just to see the journey through,
With the patient wait, knowing that we made it through.

FULL OF LIFE

Full of life you were created.
Nurtured with time,
You became the one I desired:
Permit me to hold on to the mystery,
That inspires me,
and your charm.
That overwhelms me.
It awes me to watch you,
So grateful and joyful
Poised yet alive,
Energizing my life.
Living is something I find,
Hard to explain,
As you let me relish
In the moment,
and radiate my world.

SPEAK TO ME

Speak to me:
Let me know what moves you,
What stirs and affects you,
And why it does.
I long to ease your anxious mind,
Lighten it from hurt,
To fill it with delight:
Describe to me the passions
That churn inside,
Threatening to bubble over like honey.
Passions to meet the desires,
Passions that can be released,
With the spontaneous needs.
Controlled, and varied,
Unleash what glides through your mind,
Commanding the eyes to glisten,
Like the sun reflecting down
On a bay of crystal water.

They shape and analyze to form,
a union with each other
With what is being given and received.
Permit the fingers,
To gently sense and linger,
Tease and explore,
Boldly touching with unhurried meaning.
Do not hold back the emotions,
That emerges the heart,
To Accelerate the breathing,
To add vitality to the senses.
Reveal yourself to me,
For I will listen when no one can.
Who knows you better than I?
Who is present at your every breathing second?
Feeling you as you I do,
Knowing you as I know?
That is what I do.

HERE I AM

Here I am, alone, no one next to me:
A great distance apart
Why is it that way?
This question arises within,
as I gaze across
Watching the way,
you tickle and sooth her gently,
Meanwhile caressing me with your warmth.

From a distance,
You create a desire within me,
As I view the way the water moves,
and rolls beneath you:
Responding dreamily,
My heart races,
Bringing about a longing to be held:

Wanting to be there,
I gaze once more:
As you gradually move
Not wanting to miss a spot:
This arouses my sense,
Bringing back the yearning
To be there with someone I love:

How long must I wait, to encounter you?
How long will you wait when I am away from you?

TOUCH

When I see you,
The feelings stir:
Like a gentle breeze,
Swaying my insides
Making my heart
and my knees weak.

When we touch
The sensations race:
Like a fire out of control
Inflaming my insides
Leaving my mind
in turmoil as well as my soul

When we kiss
The liquids flow :
Like a thunder bolt
Shaking my insides
Leaving my mouth
and my body needing more.

When we love
The pleasures soar:
Like electric surges
Igniting my insides
Making my body
warm with desire in stages.

MEETING

When we meet:
It is like two roads at an intersection:
Merging and blending into one,
Like the sky meets the ocean
At the end of the horizon.
When we touch:
It is like a lightening up a candle,
Glowing, melting, and burning brighter,
Giving off warmth
Like when you hold me tight.
When we embrace:
It is like two magnets joining to form a pair:
Clinging and holding together like glue,
But with some flexibility
For us to do what we want to do.
When we part:
It like opening a doorway:
Allowing ourselves to come and go,
Leaving and returning with knowledge
And experiences that helps us to grow.

AS YOU SAY IT IS

Yes, I believe you are right.
Beauty is within:
Let it take flight.
Fluttering on the wings of a dove
Shining brightly like stars in the sky
Lightening up the cloudless night.

Let my beauty be heard:
Speaking eloquently with words of prose
Lyrically set to rhyme poetically,
Ringing with timbre in my voice
With a melody that sets me free,
Resounding on every word.

Allow the beauty to glow:
Radiating gracefully from the face
Smiling tenderly or laughing with joy
Brightening the day any old way
Yes, beauty is out, from within,
As you say it is So.

YOUR PRESENCE

Your presence is perceived:
As not to hinder my path,
You calmly float,
In the mist,
to protect me,
To soothe, and add comfort,
as I think.

How else can you be felt?
When troubles arise,
You are quick to blanket me,
As gentle as a lamb,
To shield me.

My senses are attuned,
to anticipate you,
Which will cool me,
the only way, you could.
I am never without
your presence
In the reality that abounds:
On the simple days or
On the more vibrant ones.

You arise to my vision,
Emitting your splendor
To the things that are present,
and acquainting in me,
With what is relevant:
About things taken for granted.

How else to make me appreciate?
What I have
But to focus my soul
On things that are not seen
Even though right there:
When it is obstructed.

SUCH SILENCE

Such silence, preludes thee:
With no sound or sight
You materialize to me:
Be it day or night.

Your presence soothes me:
With you silent white,
You blanket me,
So tender and light.

Undisturbed, you lay before me.
As I contemplate the sight
Wanting to treasure what I see,
Before the moment takes flight.

Such tranquility moves me:
With the flow so right
The scene stirs in me:
A feeling of wondrous delight.

So quietly, So free:
You fall so light,
Please me, enlighten me,
Make the moment bright.

Your touch thrills me:
So gentle, yet with such might
To evoke in me
A quick feeling of incite.

The vision I commit to memory:
One of many I hold tight:
Each imprinting significantly
To recall when you are not in sight.

In silence you depart from me
With no sound or sight
You evaporate to be,
An element I envisioned in white.

THE ORANGE

Let me discover the hidden pleasures,
Under your protective shield,
Reveal to me your treasured treats,
That would gratify my inner needs.

What should I do now?
That my sense of touch is appeased,
Should I observe and be satisfied?
By what you have just released.

Your aroma has taken control of me,
Intoxicating all reason of thought,
Leaving me anxious and thirsty
Desiring to taste what I so long sought.

As the juices flow in me
Allow me to savor the sweet,
To taste and absorb with all my senses,
The delightful pleasures of your treat.

With each taste I partake
I linger and reflect,
On each refreshing discovery
That invigorated my senses to connect.

VISION

Who would have thought that my eyes,
could behold such a vision,
Which I would have missed entirely
if I was not thinking that opportunities are shown,
and can be present, without invitation:

So naïve was I, on that cold day,
purposely rushing along without clarity,
Lacking sight or intuitive awareness,
I almost missed the splendid display,
That captured my peripheral visibility.

You should have told me,
to open my eyes and look around,
So not to miss the simplicity of wonder
or tranquility of splendor,
That nature has abounded.

To my delight, I must reveal,
the unexpected wonderous flowing stream
of sparkling water, silently cascading
silently shimmering in the sunlight
Causing me to stop, and enjoy, the beautiful scene.

YOUR LIFE

Look at life through the petals of a Flower,
Opening each day
Blossoming, absorbing the rays,
Blooming, brightening the days.

See your life through the rays of the Sun,
Rising each day
Bursting for the light through the dark
Brightening and full of spark.

Feel your life through the steady beating of the Rain.
Falling, cleansing the day
Energizing as you deal with the tide,
Invigorating, uplifting your pride.

Explore your life like the tides of the Ocean,
Constantly racing to greet each day,
Flowing freely with renewed hope
Balancing our emotions as you cope.

NATURE

YOU

You are a tree:
A tree that is strong
With strength that flows from within
To make you flourish like blossoms do.

The kind of tree you are,
Is an evergreen,
One that is fragrant and minty green.
That shelters and nurtures,
Those that encounter you.

Like a tree:
You branch up and out,
With limbs
Covered with leaves to meet the needs.

Like a tree:
You are unlike the others around,
That go bare and life-less,
When the seasons come and go.

To me you are a tree:
Like the ones with lots of fruits
To supply and distribute,
Just the right amount and more.

THE ROSE

I stand by watching you,
Like a butterfly,
patiently waiting
for its young to mature:
Suddenly you begin to stir.

As your petals slowly open.
And you unfold in sequence,
I can see you clearly,
Like the rainbow
after the rain has ceased.

Your rich color
is displayed proudly,
Allowing the sun to adorn you:
As your beauty overwhelms
my vision to a new level.

Wanting to take you,
from your stem
I refrain from my goal,
reflecting on the moment,
Thinking that your beauty will fade.

I will have of admire you,
Seeing you as I did,
Freezing the captured vision
And committing it to canvas
I will leave you, to flourish.

TREES: THE SEASON

Your blossoms,
Watch them cluster about the branches,
As your leaves dominate the scene:
Like bees on a hive.
Look at how the colors change from light to dark,
Like a sunset leaving, as not wanting to be seen.

See how the raindrops collect on your leaves:
Like tear drops flowing from unhappy eyes.
Watch them weep with the weight,
As the sun reflects the droplets,
With a twinkling glow,
Like the stars in the sky after sunset.

You transform:
As the seasons brings you to a pause,
Like a journey coming to an end too soon:
With a collage of colors,
Appearing with a distribution of uneven balance,
Like a kaleidoscope producing exquisite views.

Now the leaves disengage as if despised,
Like fireworks separating from the main core:
You are now vulnerable and bare.
See the beauty you created dispersed,
As you stand dormant, but still alive,
With the promise, of new life to come.

BLOSSOMS

Shower me with your Blossoms,
as I walk.
Inhaling your scent,
Feeling the softness,
Watching them slowly fall
As the wind floats them
Cascading abundantly and lovingly,
Surrounding me, covering me,
as I walk.

Flower me with your petals,
A gift only you can give,
Without me asking
Revealing to my senses
To the simple beauty
as I walk.

Cover me with your fragrance,
As you shed your burden
To enlighten and add to my day,
By replenishing and opening
the awareness in my eyes
as I walk.

THE BUTTERFLY

Look at the beautiful sight,
When it moves closer to me:
Look at the texture,
As it hovers over me.
I want only to touch,
To feel the smooth softness,
To feel and caress,
As you flutter around and rest.
Come rest by me:
To be nestled and to keep warm:
Stay for a while:
And enjoy a moment of calm.
When you take flight,
My eyes will hold you in,
To memorize the place
Where you have just been.
Now you have soared,
And experienced the thrill,
Treasure the feelings,
And return at will.

FLOWERS

Flowery, Florescent,
Fragrantly releasing your essence:
Blooming and absorbing the rays,
Blossoming and brightening the days.

Luxurious, Luminating,
Learning how to appeal to the eyes:
Brightening the light and full of spark,
Bursting the way through the dark.

Openly, Opulent,
Oblivious to your beauty
Wonderous, displays of vibrant shades,
Welcoming all that transpires before it fades.

Refreshingly, Resonating
Radiant when you bloom:
Flamingly and splendid on display
Flamboyant and radiant in every way.

CHRISTMAS

This is the season to be joyful and giving,
One that is celebrated and enjoyed with the living,
It is a time to give thanks for what we can share,
A time to be grateful and to show we care.

It is the season when gifts are bought,
And given out to commemorate a once precious thought,
It is a time to come together and share,
A time to reflect and remember we care.

In this season we allow our emotions to show
And reveal treasured moments that make us glow,
It is a time we get together and share,
A time to put differences aside and care.

This is the season when a single act means so much,
One that requires a listening soul or a gentle touch,
It is a time when knowing what to do and how to share,
A time when we must let the others know that we care.

STAR-1

Full of energy you were created:
Matured with time,
You became the one to be observed:
Permit me to revel in your glow,
That inspired me,
and your brilliance,
That overwhelmed me,
From a distance.
It awes me to watch you:
Radiating the night skies,
And energizing the heavens.
As you twinkle
Let me relish for one moment,
To enjoy the sparkle, you emit.

STAR-2

Why do you cajole me?
Into a realm of confusion and delight?
Knowing that my senses
Are unused to such splendors at night.

You were sent to dazzle me,
Into a phase of utter bliss,
Taking my mind to places
That never I knew could exist.

Why do you bewilder me?
Into a state of curiosity and awe?
Knowing that my senses
Would be baffled by the sights I saw.

Were you sent to captivate me,
Into a sense of wonder and charm,
Knowing that my mind
Could be tamed and be safe from harm.

Why do you transform me?
Into a being that is charming and free?
Knowing that my senses
Would be filled with creativity.

You were sent to me,
In waves to entice my sensitivity
Knowing that my life
Would always be filled with diversity.

OCEAN

As I slowly open my eyes
I want to gaze upon you,
As you arrive and depart
I want to observe you.

Show me how you cope!
With the burdens that you bear,
Show me how you exist!
With the world so full of fear:
As you gently roll to and fro.
Let me leisurely watch you,
As you come and go
Let my mind embrace you.

As you lash out blindly,
Let my thoughts calm you,
As you rise and fall,
Let my presence comfort you:

Show me how you control.
The conflicts that you face,
Show me how you survive alone,
In the vast and open space:
Show me how you maintain,
the turmoil that is inside,
Show me how you suppress.
All the things that you hide.

Let me be in your sight.
As your struggles come to an end
Let me be warmed by you!
As you flow in and out again.

SNOW

So softly you fall,
You flow:
Why the rush?
Let me know.
Let me catch you,
Before you go.
Stay for me,
As you are
Be you:
Do not change.
Yet, you transform,
From white to ice
From ice to water
Then you flow
You go.
Where to
I do not know.
Next time
When you fall
I will watch,
To see
The beauty
To know,
That as you flow,
You show,
What you want
Me to know.

THE FOG

Unaware
You emerge in it,
You hesitate,
As you encounter it.
Suspicious
You pause,
Studying its position
As it hovers like a snake
Silently.
You wait,
It approaches,
Then it surrounds you.
You feel nothing,
Yet its visible,
You embrace it,
But capture nothing.
Again,
You watch,
As it floats around,
You reach,
Embrace,
But nothing is seen.
Uncertain,
You enter,
Like a dream
It surrounds you.

THE RAIN

I gaze around anxiously,
Trying to envision you with my eyes,
When you appear to dampen my body
With your soothing drops
That are so tender and comforting to me.
I reach out,
As you rain and pour drenching my body
with your precious drops
That are gentle to me.
I then reach,
Trying to catch you in my palms,
When, effortlessly, you shower me,
Soaking my body with your drops
That are warm and sensuous to me.
I surrender willingly,
Absorbing your gift with my entire being
Wordlessly accepting
As you cascade me with your drops
That relaxes and pacifies me.

CLOUDS

The rhythmic motion of your being
Swirling, floating,
Captivates and soothes me,
Transforming my soul, myself
Into part of you.

You look so soft so smooth,
And comforting as you move
Unrestricted in the air with all.
You tend to vary,
In size, in shape, in color.

Some days
You are hardly there,
Nothing in sight,
But There.
Other days
You are in abundance,
Moving rapidly uncontrolled
As if being chased.

Or you seem stationary,
Lying dormant untroubled
As if waiting for someone.
Then you become so discolored,
Revolving over and over,
Becoming enraged
As if you will explode.

Only if I could reach out,
To touch your fluffy banks,
Climb and snuggle in your formation,
I would know more about you.

MOON

Difficult it is to explain to someone,
How your presence affects me:
You tease me with a peek,
Occasionally exposing a view
Pretending to play hide and seek:
For some reason you appear
Willingly, yet so hesitantly,
As I patiently await you,
When all that I want revealed, is you:

Why does your presence move me?
As I am mesmerized by your sight?
You reveal a full view, occasionally:
Tell me, why do you not show me,
your true self frequently?
When all else seems cloudy,
You make the darkness right:
No matter where you happen to show.
The night belongs to only to you.

I find it difficult to understand,
Why your presence inspires me,
And enlightens me unlike others do.
You invigorate me ten-fold:
Occasionally illuminating a view
Are you aware of the power you hold?
Creating a tremor in my soul?
For with you in sight,
All I want to do, is contemplate and stare.

Your vision delights me,
when your presence creates a glow
Captivating me with the light you show:
Frequently, I gaze upon you and ponder,
That I absorb the present scenery with wonder.
You tend to obscure your view,
Hindered with clouds of white.
Why do you pretend to be so alone?
As you move about so hauntingly?

I ask why your appearance fluctuates,
Like a chameleon protecting you.
Whether quarter, half, or whole,
They are enough to keep me lured.
The many visions I witness are true,
To let your radiance illuminates the night,
Like a beacon to provide sight.
As you appear and depart, I prepare,
For the next encounters when you appear.

WATER

Water
    Sometimes transparent and tranquil
    So solid, frigid, and cold
    Like ice, frozen in time
    It captures moments to behold.

Water
    Always alive and streaming
    So furious, scalding, burning and hot,
    Like a furnace about to blow
    It ignites into flames on the spot.

Water
    Flowing never stopping
    So, challenging, meandering, here and there
    Like a stream wandering for miles
    Generating astounding momentum with a flair.

Water
    Constantly on the go yet not moving,
    So fluid, and wet, yet glassy and still
    Like a pond reflecting the skies above
    It sparks inspiration with a thrill.

Water
    Ranging never ending
    So powerful, energized, stormy and bold,
    Like a hurricane wildly lashing out
    It commands respect when it unfolds.

Water
    Sometimes rough and wild
    So unpredictable, brazen, and brash
    Like an ocean wave surging high
    It dictates when it will clash.

SUNRISE TO SUNSET

Can you picture this big balloon?
Emerging without a string,
From its long nights rest
Climbing and blazing with rays
Lightening up everything,
Can you see it?
Can you see this eloquent thing?
Greeting the early birds
Bringing out their chirps
Sounding like miniature violins
Vibrating in your ear,
Can you hear them?

Watch the effects of the big balloon.
As it kisses the leaves on the trees
That were soiled from the early rainfall,
Moistened by the dew,
Leaving them glistening
Can you see it?
Can you see this magnificent thing?
Touching the tips of the blossoms
Relinquishing the fragrance
Which tingles your nose,
and refreshes your lungs,
Can you smell it?

Picture this orange ball?
Sliding Across the sky
Moving as silent as the clouds
Interacting with all that it sees
Bringing them to life
Can you see?
Can you see effects it has?
Blinding your sight as it races
Sinking like melting like butter
Sizzling into the blue green ocean
To become the sunset at night,
Do not miss it.

INSPIRED

UNIVERSE

In this Universe we must
    Take the time to:
        Treat each other right,
        Inspire good communications,
        Measure our self-worth and
        Enjoy the precious moments.

When we live our lives
    We must take the time to:
        Teach others to understand,
        Insist on the respect for each other,
        Make each day count and
        Elevate our outlook on life.

I want to say to you that:
    I took my time:
        Trusting in your expertise
        Implementing your wise ideas
        Maintaining my patient ways and
        Extracting the most out of each day.

As we try to understand life
    We must take more time to:
        Treasure what we have accomplished,
        Indulge in positive self-improvement,
        Making the day work to our advantage and
        Enjoy life every step of the way.

FULL OF LIFE

Full of life you were created.
Nurtured with time,
You became the one I desired:
Permit me to hold on to the mystery,
That inspires me, and your charm.
That overwhelms me.
It awes me to watch you,
So grateful and joyful
So, poised yet alive,
Energizing my life.
Living is something I find,
Hard to explain.
And suspenseful to me.
So, let me relish for one moment,
As you radiate my world:
Living indirectly.

MAGNIFICENT BIRD

Watch this magnificent bird:
Observe him as he is about to ascend,
Into the sky:
Look at his posture,
Witness the proudness,
In the way he holds his head:
the boldness and certainty of his stance
Reflecting his power.
Look at the expansion of his wings:
Wide open and straight.
Now watch him,
As he rises from his perch.
Powerful and majestic
Certain of his destination.

LIFT ME

Lift me up when I stumble,
With your invisible strength
And your steadfast patience:
Steady my heart when it fluctuates,
With your calming touch
Let the rhythm beat steady,
So that my journey will be enriched and fulfilled:
Guide me along the right path, with your encouraging ways,
Lift me like a bird, and glide on the invisible wind.

Fill my mind when it is empty,
With your constant knowledge,
Let your unseeing power,
Calm my nerves as it trembles:
With your ever-constant presence
Let me grow wiser with a steady pace:
Refresh my inquisitive mind, with your understanding ways,
To overcome my fears and break free,
To soar along, like a lost feather.

Build my confidence when it waivers,
With your encouraging ways.
Let my challenges be lessons learned:
Assist me with the hurdles that hinder my path,
With your patience and guidance.
Fill my tender soul when I am vulnerable and bruised.
Let your light shine steadily through me,
So that my burdens are bearable,
To lightly drift, with positivity and with grace.

RISE

This is the time for you to rise:
Rise with the wind and let go.
Rise to new heights:
Rise:
Let the winds carry you,
To break free of the bonds
To rise to a new level
Where you are free, to be you.

Let not the past hold you back:
Soar with the wind and let go,
Soar to new heights:
Soar:
Let the wind propel you,
To release the holds on your bonds
To soar to a new level
Where you are free, to find you.

Allow the future to beckon you forth:
Float with the wind and be free,
Float to new heights:
Float:
Let the wind capture you,
As you cast aside the restrictive bonds
To float to a new level
Where you can begin, to be you.

SERENITY

Serenity without sound, Like a dropped call.
Silence.
Thinking without sound, no words to intrude your Serenity.
Nothing moves, mentally you reach out, sensing nothing,
but Silence.
Silently you reflect, hoping not to be disturbed in your tranquility,
Opening, your senses that require no sound.
Let your mind go to places where it is Silent.
Let the silence heal your complex thoughts.
See the Grey amongst the Black and White.
See from a different point of view, the blended hues,
Silently.
Blend the Red days that make you Blue and extract the Green.
Silently.
See beyond the confused and befuddled state,
Still the body, let the mind be,
Silent.
Feel the rhythm of the heart beats,
Allow them Silently to propel the energy:
It keeps you going, it beats,
Silently.
Feel the blood moving, flowing,
Silently, through very part of you.
How does it flow?
Silently.

THIS DAY

This day:
    One that is yours,
To live, to give,
    To be used, to explore,
    To be used, to do more:

Enjoy this day,
    One that is given to you,
Open it, Use it,
    To be enjoyed, do not be shy,
    To be used to fulfill, at your will.

This day:
    One to make count,
Live it, Add to it,
    To be used, to escape
    To be used, to rejuvenate.

Enjoy this day,
    One that is special,
Open it, Embrace it,
    To be savored, to be measured
    To use and appreciate, to live, not to waste.

LOOK UP

Look deep, Bring out the best:
Why try to suppress,
the joy on the outside,
or the strength inside:
The strength that is holding us up
Helping us, to maintain dignity with pride:

Pride is deep, yes it is,
Why now, why not let it out,
from inside, let us not hide,
The courage that is building up
Helping us to be strong nationwide:

Look deep for the courage:
Not easily seen, not easily felt,
from inside, let it be our guide,
The power that is hibernating within,
Helping us to recharge and be glorified.

Look deep and long, for the power,
that fuels the strength and courage,
From the inside, from depths we compiled,
Which will flow in abundance,
Helping us to overcome what is long denied.

WHAT DO WE BELIEVE?

What do we believe:
Is it what we see,
Or is it what is in our hearts?

Do we believe, what was told to us?
In the laws to which we abide,
Or is it what we seek inside?

Do we believe, what we hear?
Or in what we were taught,
Or in what we wished and hoped for?

What truths do we believe?
Is it what helps us breathe,
Or is it what takes away the pain?

Hope is what inspires us,
It is what unites us,
It is what carries us through the day.

OPEN UP

Listen to me, let me be your eyes:
Show you I will, what others do not,
Know that you will be content and enjoy,
The visions that unfold, the sights that are coy.

Observe what you see, let me be your guide:
See me as I am, when others cannot,
Enlightened you will be, so delight and partake,
The vision to be behold, and the night that awaits:

Open to me, let me be your light:
Feel you I will, when others do not,
Know that you will recall, and re-live,
The feeling that unleashes, the embers that I give:

Be close to me, let me be your comfort:
Watch you I will, when others do not,
Marvel you will be, be content and surrender,
To the emotions that you will remember.

MIRROR

Life is a mirror as they say,
One that is clear to show you the way,
Is life so open and revealing?
One that is simple to read and appealing?

Life is like the first morning sunrise,
One that is uncertain and warm,
It touches your inner being,
Like a gentle breeze that is never seen.

Life is like the unexpected thunderstorm:
One that appears furious and fast,
It wreaks havoc, and clears the air,
Leaving us no worse for the wear.

Life to me is like a blank canvas,
One which you can create your own designs,
One that changes to reflect your true self,
Bringing out the colors unlike anyone else.

GRATEFUL

I am so grateful to be alive,
In this world today,
So grateful and joyful
In every way:

Living is something I find,
Hard to explain,
Because no two days
Are ever the same:

Some days I would feel,
Wild and free,
And other days
So calm and carefree.

Just like a suspense story
Life holds a mystery,
Which makes living,
So, inspiring to me.

MAKE TIME

We say we must make time:
yet we never have a formula.

We say we never catch time:
For it only keeps racing on ahead.

We can say we watch time go by:
yet we never see it leave:
and it is gone before we know it.

We try to save time:
but we never seem to have enough to give,
Or have time, to use at a later date.

Was time really here?
Or did we imagine it?
Someone must be spending it.

BREATHE

Take time to breathe:
To inhale and exhale,
To gather strength and courage
To focus and observe
The daily confrontations in your life:

Have time to enjoy,
Hourly, day, and night:
Harvesting the moments before you forget,
Helping to prepare for obstacles that arise:
Having time to heal the body and the soul:

Amass many positive thoughts.
Always remembering to give thanks.
Allowing time to relax and recharge,
Addressing the issues and concerns,
Adding balance to each day in your life.

Never take for granted,
Nonessential things that you have,
Navigating wisely through your troubles and joys.
Nurturing often your creative being,
Never neglecting the goals that you have set:

Keep believing in one day at a time,
Knowing how to reflect and not regret,
Keenly opening-up, your inquisitive mind:
Kneading the knowledge that is power and key,
Keeping you grounded in your daily life:

Shine brightly through the dark
Shedding light on the impossible tasks
Soaring above all that holds you back,
Staying ahead and remaining calm,
Successfully bringing satisfaction, to your inner core.

FREE ME

You say I am free,
    Free to be who I am.
    But how can I be free to roam?
    When I am rooted like a plant,
    grounded in the confines,
    That nourishes me, that protects me.
    How can I be free to explore?

How am I free to go?
    When I am not free,
    But if I step out?
    How do I know,
    You will not pull me in,
    to constrain me,
    to prevent me from being free.

When I am not free,
    I see no opportunity,
    With no escape from the
    Invisible bonds,
    You have set for me:
    So, I will free me,
    Spiritually.

TODAY

Today is: A moment in time:
A part of our lives which we enter,
A part of our lives which we lived,
We took, we treasured, and Imprinted to the mind.
Only to leave behind.

Our life is a scene, and a moment in time,
Where we learn to observe
Where we savor and reflect on
How to moderate the pace, on the things
Which were out of reach.

Tomorrow is: An uncertainty in time,
A part of our lives which may come,
Which will bring challenges and enjoyment,
To planned and unplanned circumstances.
Of anticipated events.

We live: With the uncertainties of time:
Where we will learn from our triumphs of
What we had looked forward to with fear
To be fulfilled with what we wanted
And embrace what we experienced.

LIVE NOW

Live now, enjoy today:
What it brings
What it gives
What you see
Just live your life, be carefree.

Speak now, let it out and say,
What you feel
What you wish
What you hope
Just shout it out, you will cope.

Life is now, not in the past:
Live it well!
Live it now!
Live and learn.
Just live it up and take your turn.

Remember now, it is the time:
To live your life
To live and enjoy
To live, not exist
Just embrace the day and mean it.

LIFT YOURSELF

Lift yourself up,
Like a feather floating into the wind
Floating unhindered by weight
Carefree without the stress
To weigh you down.

Let your spirits soar,
Like clouds flowing gracefully above
Moving sedately without care
Slowly moving, evading the storm
That causes you despair.

Let your mind be free,
Like water cascading
Blindly falling, freely flowing
Confident in the path it takes,
To overcome the hindered restraints.

Rise to the top,
Like the mist hovering over the hills
Silently moving, regally levitating
Eluding the reaches of fear
That threatens to keep you back.

NEWNESS

The day brings with it, many revelations and hope,
It is the day we wish for to see how to cope:
Sometimes the days are easy to analyze,
Other times they are not what we realized.

We try to be open to the new challenges we face,
Hoping that our efforts would be taken with grace:
Your entrance in sight, day in and day out,
Appears right on time, without a doubt.

We greet the day with new goals in mind,
Wishing that the progression would be simple and kind:
Are you afraid of the effect, your presence brings?
What should we expect from your everyday things?

Thinking about the new people we meet,
We hope that our encounters will not be bitter but sweet:
Changing our outlooks, not confusing the mind,
Every new sight will be revealed with patience in time.

We try to hang on to what we cannot seem to grasp,
Because we want to make the moments linger and last:
When it is not bright, the sadness roams free,
Appearing in day light, brings joy we can easily see.

As the day ends, many things are left undone,
We wish the next day when it comes, we will champion,
To lend clarity to the day, to be used when we choose,
Assessing the timeline, to contemplate our next moves.

COPE

You must find a way to release tensions on the mind,
When you feel at the end of your rope,
fed up and madly confused,
Try finding and searching for hope.

Seizing the things that function best,
Is to let go and live in the moment,
Leaving the unpleasant things that prolong the past,
Which restricts what is irrelevant.

I know you feel disappointed and let down,
When expectations are not met,
You should control things within yourself,
Finding ways to release and not be upset.

Create an environment when uncertainty lurks,
And do the things you choose within,
If and when you want to get away,
Rise above what undermines your regime.

Step back in the compounds, when difficulty sets in,
And dismiss the things that dampens your day,
Calculate the aspects with a new attitude:
To find a place where things evaporate away.

BE INSPIRED

Be inspired.
Inspired by the things passing through,
    by us and about us:
Be inspired by what we are experiencing,
    in us and among us:

Be not be denied.
Denied of what was meant,
    for us and in us
Be not be denied of the missing comforts,
    in us and among us:

Be inspired.
Inspired to do more for ourselves,
    for us and in us
Be inspired by what we can do,
    in us and among us:

Be not be denied.
Denied of the things we are capable of achieving,
    with us and for us
Be not be denied from what unites us inside,
    in us and among us.

EACH DAY I AWAKE

Each day, I awake:
To hear myself and take a stand,
To hear the differences that clash and collide,
To hear the sounds that life emits,
To hear the day, not knowing what mysteries abide.

Each day, I awake:
To watch myself and take a test,
To watch the emotions that appear, recede, and progress,
To watch the transformation that life designs,
To watch the day, not knowing when I will digress.

Each day, I awake:
To control myself and take a break,
To control the feelings that fluctuates in and out in haste,
To control the turmoil that life displays
To control the today, and wonder about tomorrow, when I awake.

HEART ACHE

You will be strong:
Even though the mind is weak.
You will be strong:
You know what you seek.
The hurt, yes, is real,
The pain, yes, you feel,
The anger, yes, is there,
That why, you are still here.
You will heal in time,
Even though at times
You know the cost,
You seem lost.
The hurt, will subside,
The pain, will be less,
The anger, will cease,
When will it?
My heart is heavy.
You ask, "How much does it weigh?
What did I add,
To feel the burden
For it to pull me down
To a place so low.
I say, "Where else should I go?
It complicates the heart.

Can it break?
Can it shatter?
How can a heart break?
If it does fracture
Will it fall into pieces?
That it is impossible to mend:
If it does mend,
Will it shatter again?
In the same place?
In the same way?
Does it leave a scar?
To show it was broken?
Who will want it,
Knowing it was fractured,
Over and over again:
When will it heal,
How to make it strong?
To handle the pressures
To bounce back
To beat
To heal
The right, that was wrong?

NO MORE

I am not what you think,
nor will I be,
what you want me to be.
Who am I ?
I am finding me.
Yes I am.
I am not a door mat,
One to be stepped on,
Or trampled:
One to be wiped on,
Or dirtied:
One to be walked over,
Or ignored:
Or, one to be tossed aside,
or disregarded.
I am me,
the one that I want to be:
I am who I am.
Yes I will find me:
Yes I will,
so will you,
But now
Is not the right time.

GOALS

What are goals without the desire,
to guide us towards the spot-light
To prepare us for the roles.
which we are blinded to,
Which is life's candlelight.

What things we know to be true,
Makes our aims rise to a new height,
To help us achieve and prosper,
With things we want to do,
When we want to shine bright.

What is life worth without our voice,
To speak our thoughts out-right,
And listen without speaking out of context,
With the things we learn to overcome,
And use what we have, to unite.

What is wrong with being ourselves,
And making the best of it, despite
Our limited ability to be unique,
With keeping things balanced:
Meanwhile ignoring the tensions, we invite.

FEELINGS

ANGER

Anger, what it tells,
What it means,
It relates in expression, in thoughts, and deeds.

To all it is different:
If ignited, anger builds like a headache.
The breathing accelerates, the eyes dilated, face hardening:
Then, the anger boils and pounds.

It fluctuates to a point,
Recedes, falls, rise again, like tides,
Then overflows, to scorch all in sight.

Exhausted and appeased,
It lifts like a mist,
Only to return, to disturb the bliss.

LOVE

What is all this commotion about this thing called Love,
It is only a four-letter word that we cannot get enough of.
Love comes, Love goes, like the tide on a beach.
Love is here, Love is there, but in and out of our reach.

It is not something you can see like the white clouds up above,
It is not something you can touch like a little white dove.
Neither is it something you can hear like the beating of the drums,
Nor the sounds that come from the guitar strums.

Love is not expected like the months of the year,
But comes unannounced like the common cold you fear.
It can be short or sweet like your favorite dessert,
That you enjoy for a while, without thinking of the end, which hurts.

Sometimes Love can be long like an entire year,
Which may be just enough for you to endure and care.
On the other hand, Love is slow, Love is fast,
But I often wonder does it ever last?

Love can be like a seesaw that tends to go up and down,
Sometimes on a high, and next time on the ground.
Love can fool you; Love can rule you like the weather that is unsure,
Causing you confusion or pain, yet you still want more.

Love can be gentle and calm like the wind cooling you down,
Or wild and exciting turning you round and round.
Love is giving, Love is receiving when there is a little or allot,
It is sharing and caring with all you have got.

Love is **L**iking someone for what they are inside,
Love is **O**penness with someone with nothing to hide.
Love is a **V**erbal communication to express your desire,
And finally, Love is **E**ssential for the special admirer.

WHAT IS LOVE?

I always ask, what is Love?
Is it a sensitive topic that we mask?
Or a subject that is taken seriously and intensely,
to conquer a task.

To me: Love is a taste,
Only to be savored without haste.
To be taken delicately and carefully,
to Prevent waste.

On the other hand, can Love be seen?
Do we really know what the word means?
Or is it to be taken lightly and gently,
to infiltrate our dreams.

Is Love a feeling?
One that sends the senses reeling.
Or is it to be taken steadily and constantly,
to maintain healing.

Maybe Love is silent,
One that needs no invitation to vent:
Or is it to be taken moderately and sparingly,
to prolong the intent.

I think Love has many faces,
Like a day that dawns in various places
It is to be taken freely and openly,
to include all races.

DREAMS

You feel breathless and jittery,
Unable to remain motionless,
Unable to focus your mind intellectually:
It is there.

Without an invitation,
it filters through by osmosis,
Weighing you down and feeling blue:
Then it occurs.

What is it presuming to be?
If you know not what it is?
What term do you bestow upon it?
With its multipliable definitions:

It is not observable to the eyes,
However, its presence is sensed,
Yet I cannot identify it,
So, I become tensed:

It is not a thing:
It is feelings of:
Destinations without goals
Limitations without boundaries
Creativity without progression
And presumptions with delusions:

It arrives in variations,
Sometimes in colors
How long it prolongs, it depends,
It is ambiguous.

FRIENDSHIP

Friendship is a bond,
That can be short term or long,
No matter the distance, the bond is strong.

This invisible bond
Stretches near and far,
creating a link, never weakening,
Developing over time.
A bond that binds,
A bond that holds,
Maturing with age, strengthening with time.

Friendship is a link,
One that is invisible yet seen:
One that rekindles,
One that connects,
To bridge the distance, year after year.

With no words, it speaks,
With no ears it hears,
Friendship is a bond,
A bond, that will always be here.

QUESTION?

Question I do
About the complexity of life
So simple a thing
Yet confusingly, challenging:

So, I try
To prepare
For the diversity that transpires
Yet oblivious to the
Simplicity of the task,
Which confuses the mind:

Uncertain I feel
By the vulnerability inside,
So easily misguided,
By the perplexity,
Trying to balance the inequality at hand:

Trust I should
In the ability of the soul
To bring serenity and tranquility,
With each breath I take
To the beating heart.

TIME

Time, we know will not wait, for anyone, not even two,
We want it to wait, for the stolen moments that are few:

I recall as I wait, what we always go through:
While I lay and wait, and let feelings race through:
I know that I must wait, for its s the only thing to do,
Know that you also wait, for me to accept you as I do:

What comes to mind as you wait for me to return to you?
Life is one where you wait for good things to come to you:
Do you mind the wait, as you think of us two?
Recalling as you wait, the pleasures we hope to come true:

The excitement, is worth the wait for the many things we want to do:
How I love to prolong and wait, to know you enjoy what I do.
Each new day is a wait, just to see life come through,
The tough times are when we wait, to bring joy and excitement anew.

SIMPLY PUT

Who am I?
In the realm of
Where,
What,
When or
Why?

Where do I fit in?
As to
What I am supposed to do,
And where should I be?

Who is to say,
When I am to do these things
And Why?
What say do I have,
When things should be done.

Whom do I ask?
When all I want to do is to
Just see Eye too I.

JOY-1

What is Joy you ask?
Just a three-letter word,
What is Joy to you or me?
Can be out of this world:

We show Joy to each other.
To create feelings within,
Then the Joy that we get
Makes each day worth living:

The word Joy seems simple,
But it is complex and neat.
Simple Joy creates an atmosphere.
That makes living a treat.

I hope that these words,
Brings a bit of Joy that is true,
For it gives me Joy to create a prose
To share with a person like you.

JOY-2

A feeling unlike no other
The kind of thing that people seek,
It could be sort, near or far,
Or all over, which is unique.

Such a simple thing yet complex,
An item we all search and look for,
In things or people, we know,
Or in our daily lives where we go..

One can bring Joy to you.
However, it cannot be bought,
Joy is something we learn to achieve,
Not a simple lesson that is taught.

Joy comes in a second,
From the simplest things we see,
It can last a moment or more,
Depending on how our emotions agree.

Events can evoke Joy,
Which can be eventful and long,
It can come unannounced,
By just listening to a song.

Just an act of simple kindness from one
Illicit feelings of Joy,
Bringing out moments of well being
When the tough times deploy:

Also, from inside oneself
Joy is so much alive,
By greeting each day as it comes
We are pleased to have survived.

Joy I have learned,
Is not the same for you or me,
Joy from within is given,
To be shared at any degree.

I REMEMBER

I remember,
The moments we shared,
Are ours to retain,
Ours to reminisce,
And ours not to forget.

I recall,
The hesitating at first
The trembling touch,
The assertiveness
And the confidence that followed.

In time,
We gave of ourselves:
The knowledge we had,
The understanding
And the unselfish love.

In return,
We accepted with openness,
New experience
Different values
And mutual affection.

What I remember
No one can duplicate,
Nor can they erase,
What took place,
Nor will they come close.

The patience
We took with each other,
We built with love,
Withstood obstacles
And no one can equal it.

SENSES

See me as I am,
Not what you want me to become.
See me through eyes with no blinders:
See what I display.
Do you see the whole picture?
Made of many pieces?
The one I painted on canvas for display?

I know you sense my presence,
Sense the complexity,
Study the intricate designs.
Sense what I portray:
Do you see the individual pieces?
Working as a whole?
The ones I project every day.

Listen to what I say,
Not what you think I should speak.
Hear the words with both ears:
Listen to what I convey.
Do you feel the effects?
Silently flowing, unique and diverse?
Like the ones I write for poetic prose.

Try to understand me from within,
Understand the diversity,
Accept the given,
Understand who I am.
Do you feel the fragments?
Gradually blending, forming into one.
The ones I hope, I will not transpose.

YOU ARE AN ELEMENT OF ME

You are an element of me,
Your presence and function
Perplex me:
You arise when I need you,
And when I do not
You assure me, and provoke me,
And guide me.
In moments of grief and anger
I have no restrains over you,
I do not want to.
I allow you to pour untamed,
To eliminate my pains,
Alleviate my hurt and frustrations,
And to renew my strength.
As you repetitiously
Simmer and replenish,
And flow again.
You numb my emotions,
To bring me solace.
Then without a visual trace
You recede momentarily,
Permitting my confidence to be restored,
and my composure to be regained,
Returning boldly
To flow unashamedly
Expressing my joy.

I AM A PUZZLE

I am a puzzle:
That has just fallen apart.
Jumbled, displaced,
Where do I start?

Shall I focus from within
To soar up and outwards
Like a bee?

Shall I concentrate on the edges,
Centering downwards like a hole?
From inside out
Outside to in?
Where do I begin?

I try fitting the parts together,
Different shapes, different sizes.
Nothing matches,
Parts missing,
Unfamiliar pieces mixed in,
Confusion arises:

Where do I look to find?
What I seek to know
When I do not know
What I should be looking for?

TREASURES

Treasures:
Not the precious stones.
They are the encounters we come upon,
The fleeting moments we hold on to,
The beating hearts racing with elation,
Shining bright with each meeting.

Treasures:
The ones that the eyes will capture,
Not to covet and hide away,
But to share and enjoy,
To cry and laugh with,
To admire what is put on display.

Treasures:
What do we do when?
The encounters we have are no more,
The bonding and the time we spent:
Are saddened with the loss the aching heart?
Dimmed to a flutter, at the parting ways.

Treasures:
They are the rare ones the eyes captured:
Wanting to hold on, not letting go,
What we once shared and enjoyed.
The laughter, now bringing tears,
To what we can say, we once had.

I AWAKE

I awake, uncertain of the paths to take,
I look out.
Eager to face you again,
With me not seeing you.
I happily bring my thoughts alive.

Too often, to perfect my every move,
I look back,
With the thoughts of seeing you,
Knowing you will be pleased to see me,
I pray that the memories carry me through.

I pause, not knowing what I must face:
I look ahead,
Without you is in my life
Remembering the past moments,
I hope that the reality will come true.

Willingly, to accept the decisions I make,
I look inside,
With thoughts of you being here with me,
About the days I will treasure with delight,
Realizing that the moment is clearly in sight.

TRANQUILITY

I love those few minutes of tranquility,
When I can forget everything around me.
I think of happiness and peace,
Because it is the only thing
that puts my mind at ease.
At times like this,
I like to be alone,
To feel different matured and grown.
That is when I feel protected and free from all danger:
Because I think there is not anything,
I cannot conquer.
When I am like this,
I want to walk in the rain,
Where I feel free from all sorts of pain.
The trouble is, these moments go by so fast,
That I go back to feeling so lonely and lost.

LONELINESS

Loneliness is not genuine:
It is not a nice thing,
But it is one of the things the world must bring:
If you have found it,
what are you to do?
Just sit back and wait until it is all through.
Loneliness can be losing a good friend,
And you feel as if it is the end.
But do not you worry,
people are there,
Just waiting to care:
So, when loneliness has you caught,
Do not give it any thought.
Just wait until it has passed you by,
So, you can tell it good-bye.

I SEE YOU

I see you:
I know you:
The one with the eyes
That looks out,
To reflect in
And project out,
The things that you feel.

You see me:
You know me:
The one behind the face
That reflect out,
The wonders from within
That burst out,
To let the day, begin.

I see you:
You see me:
The one with the smile
That radiates out,
The emotions within
Wanting to shout
Where do I fit in?

You see me:
I see you:
The person on the inside
That shines out,
The one with the grin
Afraid to let it out.

SEE WITH YOUR EYES

We see with our eyes:
   The blue skies
   The blue seas
   Or what we believe
   What we want to see.
Yet we shun with our minds:
   The rain that pours, too wet,
   The sun that shines, too hot,
   The day that comes, too soon
   Not perfect, for what we had hoped.
Nothing prepares us in our daily lives:
   How to weather the storm,
   When the ship is rocking wildly:
   How to handle the downs
   When we are riding high,
   How to see Green
   When we are in the red?
Will we ever be satisfied?
   Be blessed not stressed,
   Be pleased not displeased,
   Be elated not deflated,
   And appreciate that we are here today?
Enjoy the given when it comes:
   For some, a little is better than nothing,
   For half is better than most
   For most, failing is better than not trying,
   Which are experiences with lessons learned.

BLESSED

Blessed we are,
In more ways than one.
Stressed we are,
When things go wrong.
Blessed we are,
When we meet people,
who care:

Stressed we are,
When we are not treated fair.
Blessed we are,
to embrace,
The many blessing
that flow our way.
Blessed we are,
to learn,
How each day is rare:

Stressed we are,
With the things that seems far away,
Blessed we should be,
With today, that we see:
And not stressed,
with tomorrow,
The uncertainty.

LISTEN

Listen, do you hear my words?
As they flow across your ears
Like dew drops falling off the leaves
As the sun rises to brighten the day:
Softly, tenderly, causing you to sway.
Tell me what you hear?
As my words escapes from me.
Do my words soothe you?
By the gentleness
Or do they move you to be bold:
Tell me what you hear?
When the words rush out like a raging river
Swiftly, flowing, carrying you in its path.
Do the words inspire you?
Are they strong, are they forceful?
Do they take you on a journey?
Tell me what you know,
So, my words will continue to flow,
Warmly, tenderly, only to show,
The paths brightly lit.
Do my words guide you?
Clearing the way for inspirations
To disperse from the mind and head
What must be clearly said.

REST

Rest you say:
Should I?
In your arms:
I feel comforted,
You embrace me,
You calm me,
I am safe.
You say not to worry,
but I do:
So, you soothe me,
I am comforted.
My mind is jumbled,
You must see the clutter:
Things I should let go,
Too much to let go.
Rest you say,
Why must I?
With your arms
Open wide
You hold me.

I feel blessed,
I feel comforted,
You uplift me.
My life is perplexed,
You must see the confusion:
Things of the past
that should go,
I feel lost,
You locate me:
I am soothed.
I tend to look back,
When I am in limbo:
Which things should I let go?
Rest you say,
When?
You will let me know.

BEAT FOR ME

Beat for me,
Like a Drum
Sounds without words:
Beating with a Tempo
To move the heart
Beating
To move the feet
Beating
To move the soul
Beating
Just for me alone.

Beat for me,
Like music to the ears
Sounds to create Rhythm:
Pulsating
To erase the thoughts
Pulsating
To excite the mind
Pulsating
To maintain the heart
Pulsating
To create a work of art.

Beat for me:
Like the flow of the wind
Blowing blindly with no direction
Pumping
To sustain the Rhythm
Pumping
To heighten the senses
Pumping
To keep the pace
Pumping
Just to stay in the race.

Beat for me,
Like the sea without end
Rising with abandon
Flowing to a crescendo
To its own beat
Flowing
To a cadence with no limit
Flowing
Knowing the beat is mine:
Flowing
To the Rhythm of time.

DO YOU

Do you lose reason?
Do you question why?
Holding on to
What?
The moment
When we awake
When we move
When we think
About how we live?

Do you feel it?
Do you see it?
Looking around
Where?
It is the moment:
When we see
When we hear
When we feel
What we care about.

Do you know it?
Do you believe it?
In the depths of despair,
When?
This Moment
When we choose the path:
When we choose the day,
When we choose the time,
To reflect on ourselves.

Do I know the sign?
Do I know the purpose?
To reflect on
Why?
This is the moment,
When we know
When we grow
When we show
What we do in life.

HOPE

Is there hope when one feels despair?
What is one to do,
With so much burden to bear.

Is there comfort when on feels alone?
Where is one to go,
When one is far away from home.

Is there trust when one feels betrayed?
When is one to know,
What is real and what is overplayed.

Is there belief when one feels slight?
When is one to know,
What is false without a constant fight.

Is there peace when one feels unbalanced?
What is one to hold on to,
When life is a continuous challenge.

Is there a calm when on feels anguish?
Why is one so confused,
When they do not care and act selfish.

There must be an end to the chaos that has begun:
For one is constantly at a low
When the thrill of victory is no longer fun.

NEW LEARNED STYLES

DODOITSU-1

to the computer I went
to do my work, it turned on
the screen, not a welcome sight,
you need memory.

DODOITSU-2

I watch you flutter by me
on wings so new you are like
a bee, happy to be free
of the worm body.

LAI

I wanted to bake
Some cookies or cake
Or pie:
How long would it take?
Oh, for goodness sake
Should I?
My oven needs a break
From my past mistake
Oh my!

DESCORT

Seeing through the looking glass
Reflecting back at me.
Where do I go from here?
I see me
You see me
Clear as day, Dark as night
Fragmented, Complex
Life is a Puzzle

PANTOUM-1

Looking at the water
It was calling me
To jump in, to cool off
Should I listen?

It was calling me
Tempting me, teasing me
Should I listen?
I was burning up

Tempting me, teasing me
To jump in, to cool off
I was burning up
Looking at the water.

PANTOUM-2

When I awoke today
I jumped out of bed
Looking at the time
What did I forget to do?

I jumped out of bed
Rushing to clean up
What did I forget to do?
I was late.

Rushing to clean up
Looking at the time
I was late
When I awoke today.

DIZAIN

Every day you awaken me with light
bringing a new day to my starving mind.
What have you created for my delight?
Shall I pause in awe? Or try to rewind
the recollections, some, one of a kind.
You seem to know the things that bring me joy,
Bold you are to assume, but I am coy,
to your displays, that adorns my landscape,
mesmerizing, enchanting, enjoying
your fading decent, and birth at daybreak.

HAIBUN

He began peeping through the keyhole from his closed door. He could not wait for the stroke of the midnight clock. Then he would finally see:

The person they claim
Who comes down the chimney
The jolly Saint Nick.

CASCADE-1

New I am to this style
just trying to see where I fit
In the puzzle the pencil writes out.

As old thoughts confront the new,
jumbling creative ideas emerge,
New I am to this style.

With blends I never knew
And understanding how to write
just trying to see where I fit

Confusion escapes the mind
Hoping to make sense
In the puzzle the pencil writes out.

CASCADE-2

Why did you invite me?
In this crowded place
When I cannot move around.
The words I hear
Sound gibberish to me
Why did you invite me?

They speak so foreign
Talking a mile, a minute
In this crowded place.

Music loud and different,
People dancing with no care
When I cannot move around.

MINUTE POETRY

Not today my dear secret one,
I thought you gone:
Two days per chance
You had your dance.

Longing I am, for my real treat
The one with heat!
Too much to say!
Please go away.

True, you keep it cool with showers,
You bring flowers:
But the sunshine!
Is my divine.

GOLDEN SHOVEL

My soul can reach, when feeling out of sight –
Third line from Elizabeth Barrett Browning Sonata –
HOW DO I LOVE THEE? Sonnet – 43

The distance between me and my
true love, is so far, that my soul
longs and aches, for the time we can
finally make up for the long wait, and reach
the levels of E. B. Browning's understanding, when
we can better work and strengthen the feeling
of when or why, you ventured out,
creating a deep longing of
seeing you again, in my sight.

DIAMANTE

Snow
Fluffy, Cold,
Swirling, Falling, Accumulating
Blanketing the path, Slippery under foot
Numbing, Chilling, Hardening
Frozen, Wet,
Ice

DIAMANTE

Crying
Clear, Moist
Streaming, Leaking, Stinging
Salty, Streaks, Damp, Wet
Embarrassing, Pouring, Flowing
Uncontrollable, Expressive
Tears

ODDQUAIN-1

Sleep
blissful state
Silence, finally
Waited all day just for this
Rest.

CROWN ODDQUAIN

Kiss
Will it be
Repeated or not
Unsure what to feel inside
Bliss.

LENTO

Lost

Talk to me through the script again,
Walk with me and hold my hand,
Mark my words, I will be better than before,
Hark, let me know where I stand.

Give me time to correct my wrongs,
Live in me each day:
Forgive the pain, that I have caused,
Inattentive I was, along the way.

HARRISHAM RHYME

Strength

Motivation comes to us from something **denied:**
Nervous tensions surfacing from their **depths**
Swimming to new heights, all **entwined:**
Growing stronger and giving us renewed **breadths:**
Gone is the fear that once **reclined:**
Envigored, inspired, and gaining more **respect.**

BREF DOUBLE

I looked at my watch
only to see the time tick-tocking away.
It sure is taking a long time!
Impatiently, I wait for the train.

The two o'clock train was overdue
That is the one I had to catch
to make sure I was at the track on time:
I know the team's pride had much to gain.

Today was the championship match,
Everyone was counting on me:
Not that I could score all the points,
But to them, I must uphold the family name.

Winning each year was the catch.
Would I be the one to take the blame?

VERS BEAUCOUP

The Season

Gifts at the START, we IMPART, from the HEART
are a PART of the love we SHARE, to show we CARE,
So, PREPARE, we do, with ENERGY, and INTENSITY,
and VITALITY, when BLESSED and not STRESSED.

Each YEAR the tradition brings a CHEER to the EAR
yet BEWARE of the TIME we DINE
merrily drinking WINE, that makes us CAREFREE and BUBBLY,
wishing HAPPILY about the PLOY that brings us JOY.

BOP

Hand covered over my ears,
I walked up to the house
to music blasting and walls shaking.
another day of this loud noise
reverberating in my ear drums,
not the sounds I had hoped to listen to.

I did not read between the lines.

The advert impressed me:
quiet person with love for music,
needed to care for place,
at night and weekends.
Rent free plus $1000,
and not far from transport.
How can I beat that price?
when I had no job:
But the constant loud music
was taking a toll on my ear drums.

I did not read between the lines.

What should I do?
8 more months on my contract.
Will the constant noise ever stop?
Deaf I will be by the end of the year.
One night I got the nerve,
looking all smug
I entered the room with ear buds in and pulled the plug.

I did not read between the lines.

CATENA RONDO

Open up for me my flower
So long the wait, the time is now.
My eyes are anxious, your beauty awaits
Open up for me, my flower.

So long the wait, the time is now
To show your true colors
What is the probability this year?
So long the wait, the time is now.

To show your true colors
Let the sun rays flame your petals,
Come out of your cocoon
To show your true colors

My eyes are anxious, your beauty awaits
Uncoil each petal tenderly
To proudly display your creation
My eyes are anxious, your beauty awaits

Open up for me my flower
So long the wait, the time is now.
My eyes are anxious, your beauty awaits
Open up for me, my flower.

CLARITY PYRAMID

Break
Recess
Vacation
looking for a place
be free of the nine to five

"interruption of the routine"

CLERIHEW

Mickey Mouse
Disney World is your house.
Visitors from far and near,
M.I.C.K.E.Y. is all they cheer.

SEPTOLET

New Year

Eyes
Wide open
Looking up.

People huddled
staring intently
waiting for ball
to fall.

EPULAERYU

Fruit
Mango, a tropical fruit
Hanging from the tree
Yellow and ripe, succulent
Smell the aroma
Mouthwatering treat
Want to pick
Now!

VILLANELLE

*Why can you not see ME standing **there**?*
YOU, spending more time on your mobile **phone**
And ME, looking at you with my hands **bare:**

I came up to you and said, "Hi dear!"
YOU, just left me all alone
*Why can you not see ME standing **there**?*

I wanted to tell you that I can share
For I was on my own
And ME, looking at you with my hands **bare:**

It was your turn to be **aware**
When I arrived at home
*Why can you not see ME standing **there**?*

Can that phone whisper in your **ear**?
Does it hear ME groan?
And ME, looking at you with my hands **bare:**

I now realize that YOU do not **care**
Silly of ME to moan
Why can you not see ME standing there?
And ME, looking at you with my hands **bare:**

TRI-FALL

runner's anticipation

The stage for all is set
hearts pounding
fueling the blood to all
Focus on the feet, one mindset
astounding
all minds tuned in. I cannot fall..

Feet behind the start line
eyes ahead
the race path is ready, inhale
and let me hope this time
my biped
is the one first to cross the trail..
The whistle blows, we run
eager to
complete the mission and win GOLD
lots of celebration..
I just know
my NIKE is swift and well soled.

PUENTE

For Tomorrow Was Another Day.

Time was passing him by
while the season was changing
he idled and dreamed
and did not even lift a hand
when he watched others gather

~for tomorrow was another day~

he thought to himself silently
wishing and hoping he had
spent more time doing something
instead, it was too late now
he did not gather food for the winter.

CON-VERSE

Patience and Focus

Sunday in Church we did pray
Asking him to bless the day

Our thoughts were on that juicy Ham
As the Pastor's sermon dragged on

Not thinking of Lent Fish, but of meat
We fidgeted on the hard cold seat

How long to wait for breaking of the bread?
Blocking out all temptation in our head.

CONSTANZA

Realization

Music, sounds to my ears so clear
To catch up with present day mood
Melodic past will now intrude.

Many things in passing we hear
With sights playing on eyes divine
Buried visions emerge in time.

True to its form we wait, we stare
With anxious thoughts perplexed and true
Uncertain, confused, and yes blue.

Who is it that knows my real fear?
The timbre that rings with no sound
Parallels the unknown compound.

Elation brings clarity near
So, listen closely to the high
With intensity that comes nigh.

TROLAAN

We are waiting for the day
With visions of many tasty treats
Watering mouths ready to eat and say
When can we sample the different meats?

Every year families get together
Engaging in foods they rarely eat
Each one more tastier than the other
Every bite so scrumptious and sweet.

Vittles in abundance stacked on the plate
Variety all around, and moderation is key:
Vineyards supply the grape to toast the date
Vintage bottles that were full, will be empty.

Inhale, exhale, make room for more food
Inner mind says, "slow it down"
Instead, we just follow the hungry brood
Indulging until the next course comes around.

GRA REFORMATA

STEW

It is 5 am and you are ready for our date
all fluffy and white,
eager to avoid going to the plate.

you nibble at my fingers
although I have nothing to give.

Pushing open the door, you wait,
Ready to rush into the day light.
It is 5 am and you are ready for our date.

Wait for me to hold your leash,
You are too precious to get lost.

No way, I am letting you escape,
You are tugging me along with all your might,
eager to avoid going to the plate.

I see the hunger in your eyes
and thirst too, I can tell.

So sorry I am, that I was late
The time is still twilight
It is 5 am and you are ready for our date.

Come let us walk
so that you can get your fill:

Eat all that you want, I will wait
while you tug and fight
eager to avoid going to the plate.

You look so contented, grazing so carefree
Munching on the tender sprouts,

Oh, just accept your fate!
Soon, you will be a tasty, tender, delight
It is 5 am and you are ready for our date.
eager to avoid going to the plate.

FLORETTE

I saw the elders as a tot
fanning away when it was hot
under the tall windows inside
as the breeze blew over my side, why not.

They sipped on their drinks with no ice
for there wasn't a cold device
in the little house on the hill
while they just laid back and sat still, unwise.

Just you wait till you reach sixty
they said as I ran happily
around in the sun with no care
ignoring them as they sat there, misty.

Back then I was just so carefree
watching them sweat so profusely
Now I am older, I can feel
At my age, time had to reveal, duly.

WHO AM I

Blossom, Blossom
I am a Blossom,
Trying to grow up.

I am a Blossom,
Trying to grow up.

Blossom, Blossom
Bla, Bla, Bla,
So I am a Blossom
So I am a Blossom.
You are not a Blossom
I am a Blossom.

Blossom, Blossom
Blossom, Blossom
I am an older Blossom now.
So hear you people
I do not need a fairy
People I do not need a fairy no more.

By
Renee Rose

ABOUT THE AUTHOR

Born on the island of Montserrat BWI – also known as the Emerald Isle of the Caribbean. Mathematics Educator to students as well as a Track Official and mentor to all ages. Hobbies: Works on Art with still life in spare time along with creating prose. Likes to Travel, loves nature and music as well as spending time on the beach.

POEMS

PEOPLE

MY SISTER	3
RENÉE	4
SUSAN & JUSTIN	5
XAVIER	6
DOC. MAC-G	7
FATHER	8
MOTHER'S	9
DENTIST	10
MY LOVE	11
MOMENTS	12
WE KNOW	14
NICE	15
BE CONTENT	16
SPECIAL	17
I WANT TO SHARE	18

EMOTIONS

TO YOU I GIVE THIS	23
FRAGMENT	24
I AM	25
PONDER I DO	26
NO CLUE	27

HEAVY IS THE SOUL	28
CONFUSED	29
THE RETURN	30
LET ME	31
THE WAIT	32
FULL OF LIFE	33
SPEAK TO ME	34
HERE I AM	36
TOUCH	37
MEETING	38
AS YOU SAY IT IS	39
YOUR PRESENCE	40
SUCH SILENCE	42
THE ORANGE	44
VISION	45
YOUR LIFE	46

NATURE

YOU	49
THE ROSE	50
TREES: THE SEASON	51
BLOSSOMS	52
THE BUTTERFLY	53
FLOWERS	54
CHRISTMAS	55
STAR-1	56
STAR-2	57
OCEAN	58
SNOW	59
THE FOG	60
THE RAIN	61

CLOUDS	62
MOON	64
WATER	66
SUNRISE TO SUNSET	68

INSPIRED

UNIVERSE	73
FULL OF LIFE	74
MAGNIFICENT BIRD	75
LIFT ME	76
RISE	77
SERENITY	78
THIS DAY	79
LOOK UP	80
WHAT DO WE BELIEVE?	81
OPEN UP	82
MIRROR	83
GRATEFUL	84
MAKE TIME	85
BREATHE	86
FREE ME	88
TODAY	89
LIVE NOW	90
LIFT YOURSELF	91
NEWNESS	92
COPE	93
BE INSPIRED	94
EACH DAY I AWAKE	95
HEART ACHE	96
NO MORE	98
GOALS	99

FEELINGS

ANGER	103
LOVE	104
WHAT IS LOVE?	105
DREAMS	106
FRIENDSHIP	107
QUESTION?	108
TIME	109
SIMPLY PUT	110
JOY-1	111
JOY-2	112
I REMEMBER	114
SENSES	115
YOU ARE AN ELEMENT OF ME	116
I AM A PUZZLE	117
TREASURES	118
I AWAKE	119
TRANQUILITY	120
LONELINESS	121
I SEE YOU	122
SEE WITH YOUR EYES	123
BLESSED	124
LISTEN	125
REST	126
BEAT FOR ME	128
DO YOU	130
HOPE	132

NEW LEARNED STYLES

DODOITSU-1	135
DODOITSU-2	135
LAI	136

DESCORT	137
PANTOUM-1	138
PANTOUM-2	139
DIZAIN	140
HAIBUN	141
CASCADE-1	142
CASCADE-2	143
MINUTE POETRY	144
GOLDEN SHOVEL	145
DIAMANTE	146
ODDQUAIN-1	147
LENTO	148
HARRISHAM RHYME	149
BREF DOUBLE	150
VERS BEAUCOUP	151
BOP	152
CATENA RONDO	153
CLARITY PYRAMID	154
CLERIHEW	155
SEPTOLET	156
EPULAERYU	157
VILLANELLE	158
TRI-FALL	159
PUENTE	160
CON-VERSE	161
CONSTANZA	162
TROLAAN	163
GRA REFORMATA	164
FLORETTE	166
WHO AM I	167